The Facebook Status I Wish I Could Post

The Facebook Status I Wish I Could Post

Keitaris J Goldston

The Facebook Status I Wish I Could Post

Copyright, 2022

Table of Contents

The Facebook Status I Wish I Could Post

Dedicated to those who've inspired me the most: Jesus Christ, Beyoncé, Viola Davis, and Angelina Jolie. Thank you all for allowing me write so freely.

The Facebook Status I Wish I Could Post
The Recipe

1 tsp of ignored phone calls

5 cups of backstabbing

6 quarts of truth

20 pints of isolation

4 shades of depressions

&

7 tablespoons of deadly spider kisses tied by the webs of misunderstandings

Preheat the oven for 30 minutes of fuck you at

450 degrees Celsius

Bake in the oven at 450 degrees Celsius for 1 long unfortunate hour until Brown

Take out and let Your deceit cool for 20 minutes

To hell with this

Eat until you taste the hint of cinnamon and nutmeg of which one of these adds no flavor

That is how you concoct a host of sweet believable lies and betrayal

The Facebook Status I Wish I Could Post

The Alchemist

She holds my face in her soft palms. My mother the martyr for her children. He sees me in his gaze My father the wise magician. Her essence and happiness are a breath of fresh air, My stepmother the creative one.

Her shyness is an illusion for my little sister is a clever fox. Strong and free He is in California finding God instead of living life within the confines of a box. Here with us you are the strongest pillar, we call you eldest brother. Memory fading, face never frowning, I call you great grandmother

The Facebook Status I Wish I Could Post
The Burning Sands

He takes the paintbrush in his hands and paints for me the lines in the burning sands

When my silhouette is wrapped in loincloth and the wings on my back are weakened...

When my world is caving in at night and I don't know what to do in my darkest of times He paints for me lines in the burning sands

He does this for me in the middle of the night

He paints Me with his hands, and I can see him standing there in the illuminating Moonlight—a muscular back turned. He paints for me the lines in the burning sands

After making love under forest starry skies that have clocked past midnight, the morning's steamy mist rises from the mountains and float on the lake

Upon opening my eyes, I see him lying there. He's sleeping with paint all over his hands and I lift myself up to see he's painted Me in the burning sands

He thinks I don't see him peaking at me when he's supposed to be sleeping but he wants to see my face as I marvel at his painting of me. He wants me to know the work of his hands and to know he's painted me in the burning sands

His eyes remind me of honeycomb and amber rivers. His smell like dark sweet soothig cologne...My favorite Egyptian Musk with hints of fireplace. Beneath the sheers and the whispering His breath is that of peppermint. During the movies we watch, He holds me in his hands and in this state of being I remember my portrait embroidered on that the canvas. And I *knew* he'd cross sea and ocean

All that for me... He'd paint me in the Burning Sands

The Facebook Status I Wish I Could Post
Mother of Saturn& Hecate

Spirit Mother of Saturn Do You hear my crying call

Does the panting deer— who goes to the river— birth her young in warms dens where they have fresh bedding?

Goddess of the Moon, Hecate—who doesn't hear if there is anything— Does the deer prance over creeks and dance in your precious moonlight?

When you reign in the tides do they sing the Jesus walk?

Fog rises on open fields and in the dead of night owls take their flight searching for their prey that are *praying* and *preying* on one another like the snakes. The vipers hide in the grass. The lions that prey on lambs, and the hyenas that come about with their mocking laughter, come to fest upon your bones

Hecate, I call to you! Answer me Hecate!

I am running in the dead of night with the eyes of the hunter, seeing blind through the grass, and my senses are at their *zenith*. I am blind, seeing blind through the trees. They are chasing after me!

Send the tides, send the beasts of the night that prey on me to prey on the hunter that hunts me—the hunted

The Facebook Status I Wish I Could Post

Wounded prey, crying to their kind to save them, but
they never answer for fear they will be eaten

The Facebook Status I Wish I Could Post
Where are you true love?

Where's that face I'm dying to see?

Why do hips crack and emotions quake from the rhythmic ballet that anchors our power?

Who are you with this face shrouded in complete mystery? Why can't I see you?

 I awake in the morning and the space besides me is empty. At night, I align my body with the wall so at least there's *"something"* there with me until you return.

Who are you? All I can see through this cloudiness is a figure with no definite look, but in some odd way I already know it's you.

You're frightening and…You're beautiful

The Facebook Status I Wish I Could Post
Wilt

Wilting flowers in the meadow reveal your secrets.
For the first time, I wilt my body to you, and it was
"*willingly*" exotic.
I sought my body to your feet. I demanded your
respect, time, money, and patience.
I was like a child in a candy shop. AND YOU
NEVER HAD COMPLETE CONTROL. But the
other times. . .all the other times... all counted into
one total fucking blur

You were like a thief in the night.
Why? Why would you steal something that was
given to you so...so *willingly*?
You took it, ran with it, harbored it, cherished it like
a diamond and abused its luster. You fantasied
about it. And you daringly tried to use it against me.

Nigga that "*shyt*" don't even work

I say Woe to you! Cause when the time comes, the
past, present, and future will merge revealing the
light that will show everything. Just know that I
forgive you.

Cause "it" is reborn

"*Smdh*"...Yes a *Newborn*...fresh, and alive, and
moving.
Shining with life as a fresh spring shimmering in
the radiant sunlight.
"Drink from me, Drink from me, Drink from me oh
so evenly. Drink from me, o' so delicately in My
"Entirety"

13

The Facebook Status I Wish I Could Post

The taste was sweet—even when bitter
I spit out the lies from my mouth and rinsed it out so
I could finally have a *new* cup of wine
I forgive you. Forgiveness is bliss

Yes, I forgive you...indeed.
The emotions that are invoked from your unlawful
memory...I commanded you set me free...And I was

The Facebook Status I Wish I Could Post
Becoming a Born-Again Virgin

At the alter I bow down and succumb to my knees. I place three red hot chili peppers in my mouth and let the heat burn while my eyes start to tear like the Louisiana estuaries that flow into the Mississippi

I look up to the stain glass windows and ask Jesus Christ again for the forgiveness of my sins.

You might not know this process, but when I'm finished suffering, I will become like *New*

A Born-Again-Virgin

You might think this was religiously exaggerated and pointless. However, this ceremony was needed.

Jesus above all. He knows my heart

The Facebook Status I Wish I Could Post
Titles

From Lemons to Lemonade

Catching Flies with vinegar

Sand

Salt

Word for those who
are suffering in silence,

a fucking masterpiece

The Facebook Status I Wish I Could Post
Culprit

"Beautiful creature I command you" says the goddess of love.

But the ancient Egyptians had the wrong definition of mythology did they not?

Graves and cinder blocks littered with rose petals wafting deadly love into the air

Egyptian scented oils running down the gravestones and drooling into empty graves. I am surrounded by white burning candles illuminating the litter of uprooted soil

An empty casket that contained a block of ice. This block of ice contained a human heart with four chambers: Passion, Desire, Compassion, and the Will of having sacrificed time longing for your presence

A presence that wrought my chest with pressure and made my chest heave in the presence of your absence

My heart freezes and time grows faint. I paint a picture of happiness that brought darkness. And so indeed my heart wrapped itself and turned to ice

I ripped it out my chest with the best effort and concealed it in an unmarked grave that was made from the earth; The earth once void until God himself shaped it in 7 beautiful days while having defeated the Fallen

I took my heart, buried it, and covered it with ashes-to-ashes, dust-to-dust, sand-to-sand

I had final became free from you

The Facebook Status I Wish I Could Post

I was in need of forgiveness and so I dug it up, and let it defrost, and now I can move on

I've put the past behind me

The Facebook Status I Wish I Could Post
Vesuvius

I was the illegitimate child of Apollo and Minerva.

It was I, that was endowed with great power at birth. However, if I break the sacred law, I'll lose my gift. As I grew older and wiser, I was greatly admired, and I soon captured the eye of someone whose heart was on fire

Do you my friend believe in love at first sight?

I think I do. Why can't it be talked about or claimed?

I moved to and fro in the heavens like a weightless bird and our soft harmless gazes turned into an encounter. Decorative robes, given to me by my mother's most diligent hand servants were dropped with effortless effort

A crown made from Apollo's flame burned like gold, yet I was *His* silver

As my love came closer, He grew hotter, and we were soon wrapped in a passionate heat. But soon there was lightning and thunder. Apollo and Minerva themselves brought a wrath equipped with the jealously of Gods

For love was not in *our* vocabulary

My love was destroyed in an instant by Apollo's fiery grip. I was next. I had broken the sacred law...falling in love. And what made it even worse is that *'He'* was in our paradise

The Facebook Status I Wish I Could Post

An invisible force held me down as my god-like glow
started to fade; My eyes started to lose their fiery
embers. My skin turned pale like human flesh

They through me down to the earth, but instead of
the earth I was headed straight for a volcano

I muscled up any celestial energy left within me.
Fire surrounded me and I was soon in the volcanic
pit being bathed in searing hot magma

With the power left in me I raised my hands up to
the gods

The volcano erupted and lava lit the sky like a
blazing sunset for their destruction

So *much* anger...so *much* rage

In my name, Pompeii had been destroyed that day

What was the gift you ask. The daring ability to be
myself, and love who I wanted to unapologetically

The ability to start a controversial volcano

I am Vesuvius

The Facebook Status I Wish I Could Post
The Liquor

Heineken, corona, platinum

Bee thy honey whiskey in my tea

Crown, Vodka, Hennessey

Oh, look what you've done to me...

Long islands and blue motherfuckers which way is up?

Sweet Sex on the beach

Winter Warming Apple Cider walking through your mansion I'll start a fire

The Facebook Status I Wish I Could Post
God, Do You Cry?

God, do you cry when your children sin? Is that why
it rains. When it thunders and lightning rips
through the sky is it because your angry with your
children?

God why is your voice so quiet when we pray?

What is on your mind?

When there are tornados and hurricanes why do
innocent people perish?

Why do people like me have no passion to cherish?

The Facebook Status I Wish I Could Post
I feel like screaming

Lashing out at everyone

I feel like crying an ocean

What is really preventing me from driving down the
highway away from here with feelings *"cascaded"*
back after midnight

The Facebook Status I Wish I Could Post
I See

I see so many people smiling while I'm here

It's as if they know what they wanted. I know what I want but I can't see what I am grabbing for. It's like falling through emptiness into a void that is just falling; You become one with yourself again and the cycle begins again

It's like spinning around and around and around and around and around. When do I get off this crazy ride?

It eats, it's feeds, it moves, it coils, it wraps around your throat. . . you can't breathe

It's depression

The Facebook Status I Wish I Could Post
Crumble

When my life is crumbling around me

When life seems stale and gray pull me in close and
teach me not to be afraid

Feed my fire, kiss my lips, be the one that holds me
betwixt thy hips in everlasting protection that brings
a destructive reckoning force of love

Love conquered all once and it can do it again
So…when my patience is wearing thin

bear with me this the weight of our sins

Take me hand in hand

Reach inside me and set my soul a blaze

So that when I'm feeling empty and down At least I
know you'll be at my side, at least you'll be the one
who prays

At least I know you'll be the one who stays

The Facebook Status I Wish I Could Post
Universe

Beg for me

Kiss me

Lick me

Taste my inner thigh

Penetrate my universe that conceptualizes the
connection to your hypothalamus

Ease inside. Take me for a ride through your mind.
Let me into Your impenetrable thoughts...The *map*
traveling through your mental cortex, coursing, and
swerving up your spinal cord into your midbrain

For I've deceived even the darkest of minds

Envelop me in your arms that capture my riveting
forte of balance and excitement. Pass through my
ear canal and shed light on my racing thoughts that
never seem to rest

Be my relief during the times the universal entropy
is *"in heat"*

...u get my fukin' drift...if not let me know

Where the fuq are you?

The Facebook Status I Wish I Could Post
Your Swag

I just want you to know...I love your swag.

You're handsome. Your smile invoking...your lips are icy smooth, and I can only imagine...

Your kiss would Be hell of fukin' tasty right now

On my knees I would administer the deed and never Give you full control

I want you to myself because the need of my burning desire needs to *Be* quenched. Fingernails scratches etched in your back like hieroglyphics, but you will never be a pharaoh in my eyes

Because I cannot be contained

The Facebook Status I Wish I Could Post
Taj

In my peripheral vision, I see you ready to bow
down at any moment. You can't keep your silky
amber eyes off me. Your skin is ready to leap from
your bones to encapsulate my wonderful Taj Mahal;
embellished with Cocoa and Shea butters and
deliciously bathed in African scented oils

I am a sweet Tahitian tree full of melted sugar and
ivory pearls that burn in the lake of dangerous drugs
that conspired against your senses, and beckoned
the deep emotional visions of me that were concocted
and fabricated by your olfactory lobes

I see your deepest secret

"Wanting" is the secret... I am the deepest secret

Come to the Taj Mahal

The Facebook Status I Wish I Could Post
Safe Haven

Honestly...you used to be my safe haven. With open arms you invited me in, and I willing and foolishly accepted. During that time, I was a vulnerable person wrapped up in my "confusions" of what I wanted and what reality had set in place for me. I thought you were like a lovely protective entity sent from the gods bathed in nectar and ichor

You were Vital to my Vitality

I could've never wished for the most perfect person. Who else would love me, my mind, my body, my insanity, my perplexed attitude, my rough patches my temper

I have this elusive side that I've been dying and wanting to express to another human being

I thought you were the shit

With the way your Egyptian musk oils—entangled with the sweet smell of imported Arabian tobacco, only softened by the hint of coffee and peppermint— tainted your lips. They reeked of pure bliss when we were cuddle up on that bed together. I let your rose petals float in my river. They glazed my water

Ripples created by movements that were ever so slight. It was surely pure heaven I thought

Hell, no...

In actuality You were a dangerous cliff that I was willing to jump off and let you catch me. You caught me then you purposely let me go so I would fall to

The Facebook Status I Wish I Could Post

the ground. The remnants of my broken body
littered the ground and all my organs scattered to
the winds: Of course, that would've happened if I
landed. Meanwhile I'm still falling. Waiting for the
next one to catch me and this time, I'll never make
the same mistake

I was, and still am, in need of a Safe Haven

The Facebook Status I Wish I Could Post
Breathe

I breathe hate

I breathe torcher

I breathe pain

I breathe treachery

I had to breathe love in a place with no oxygen to oxygenate my lungs and you still have absolutely no understanding about the concept or depth of my sufferings

I say to you, take the sun and eat it raw so that your throat burns and eventually rots out of your body...and even then...that won't be enough repayment

Evade me

The Facebook Status I Wish I Could Post
Undergrad

Undergrad was a hard time for me. Many times, I found myself mixing benzos and alcohol to sleep. I couldn't fine the strength to eat. Feeling thy heart go beat, beat, beat against my chest. Dizzy and inebriated I would ask,

"Why am I here? Why am I here?"

The Facebook Status I Wish I Could Post
The Face of Mystery

It has never appeared to me how lovely you appear
to me, but even now you face is still an illusion

The Facebook Status I Wish I Could Post
12 pm

You haunt me by the weight of your eyes

You remind me of my father

He hides his true feelings to shun the weakness because you know it is your greatness power.

You came home late again last night

I ate honeydew melon today. With every slice I thought of you. And we both know I don't like melon unless it's 'Water'. Do you like honey dew melon? Of course you 'dew'

I washed your laundry. Your favorite shirt: Your scent still lingers like an invigorating smell that makes my teeth clench down popsicle sticks to splinters

I made dinner for you tonight. Trying to impress you in every way to make you happy. Drowning in desperation for your adoration, but all I get is your unappreciation

I took a bath today, I waited for u to drags me under the water. Your message in a bottle

Opening my eyes, I can see the ocean. Slowly i began to the lose the will to drink from You. Your garden was withering, while mine was sprouting and in bloom

You remind me of someone I forgave. I placed hot red chili peppers in between my cheeks while tears ran down my face. After my bath I laid on the couch

The Facebook Status I Wish I Could Post

nakedly cocooned in a silk robe. I drank 3 cups of
wine and fell asleep. By then it was only 11:59 am

It's your day off and you're still not home

It nearly 12pm

The Facebook Status I Wish I Could Post
Gain: The Smell of My Sheets

You make me smile when I come home

When I wake up, I awaken to the soft smell of Gain laundry detergent in my sheets. Sheets that you washed so I snuggle in them while you make me breakfast in bed. You've prepared my favorite: eggs, sausages, coffee with three creams, almond milk, and four Splenda with 2 rose petals

Laying in the bed with my hair an absolute mess you still love me. What exactly is it about me you love?

Is it that I'm clumsy, the fact that I'm quirky. My intellect?

Is it my smile or my innocent amber glowing eyes? Or is it the way my skin smells like Jasmine and vanilla musk with the hint of dark soothing sunrises?

At sunset, we go for a walk on the pier among the waves. We go for midnight swims under moonlight. Here in the water with you I am weightless and free. Sing to me like a siren our love song. Change me into a merperson with the magic of your melody. Kissing me—thyne lips like soft Egyptian cotton forged by Iranian honey and warmed by brown sugar with a hint of pumpkin spice

They taste like exquisite fresh grounded expresso from Dubai, sweeten sugar cane, bittersweet tobacco leaves and a light touch of marijuana

A kiss heightened by mystery. . . where will it lead us next my love?

The Facebook Status I Wish I Could Post
Away for the day, Then Present

Couches empty

Absence is plenty

I miss you and write poems for you because *we* exist.

I fell asleep last night on the couch writing poetry with my heavy eyes because I was just so possessed with you. Your ankles I miss

I miss your legs and your body pressed against mine.

I like the way you pick my brain and turn my pages like a book you've been dying to read. I'm that mystery novel and you are hypnotized. What's stopping you from putting me down if you really don't wanna read me

Couch empty, bed empty, bed canopy and curtains moved by the breeze of left open windows. Houses with high ceilings and long crystal hallways with chandeliers that decorate the ceilings. The unforgettable smell of fresh linen coursing through the open air

The House is quiet. . . still even. . . very still...almost motionless. I am motionless. I struggle as I play our song on my piano

The backup orchestra is my body. My ribcage a harp. My Heart is the percussion. My brain the conductor. My thoughts the musical passages varying in musical variation that imitate my sorrow developed by the longing of your absence

The Facebook Status I Wish I Could Post

My paintings and poetry are just a figment of my imagination of you. It is a deeper expression of emotions that are not well comprehended by you, highly misunderstood by other, and well I haven't really understood it all myself

My art: This ode to you is just love

It's that simple

The doorbell rings and your home with a smile on your face

You make me smile

Today I am blessed and complete

You were away and now you're here

Now your present

The Facebook Status I Wish I Could Post
Inside and out

I am a river

I am an ocean

I am the sea

A large body of water that is vast with emotion and deeper than the Atlantic and Arctic combined

But as I float in this ocean, the current is *'unmoving'*. Absolutely stagnant. As if we are now separated in time. Before we use to dance with each other in a constant pattern: *Push, Pull, Twisting, Crashing,* forming like the waves on the open seas

But now as the waves subsides into tide pools, I'm left here floating on top of stagnant waters. . . it is lifeless

The Facebook Status I Wish I Could Post
Searching. . .

. . . for You in My sheets that the wind lifts with a tender breeze

Your vibrato

The sound… The treble in your cadence, the pulse of your rhythmic choice of words. My mind like a radar searching for your lips. Nothing can stop me

You find me and grasp my hips around your waist

Large hands that held the pillars of the Parthenon

Your body chiseled like superior black onyx mirroring intricate patterns of veins

Your smile is beautiful, your skin soft and smooth

 Embedded by patterns of tattoos

You bite thy neck, and my body becomes limp and motionless while my skin evolves into goosebumps

My eyes meet the sun's rays pouring in the room through the curtains

My breaths deepening into begging moans..."*Oh my God,*" I cry into the ear of my lover

This only skyrockets the sensation

But I still…I remain searching for this prophecy.

The Facebook Status I Wish I Could Post
Where are you?

Love me inside and out . . .

I want to ask: Are you waiting on me when I come home? Are waiting for me in time? After a long day at the office, I just want to open my mind to you and divulge every thought, worry, complaint, because you understand me. . .you love me. . .you kiss me on my forehead and love me by the waist and take me for a never-ending ride through your thoughts

Where are you?

Are you waiting for me when I come home? Are you waking up in the morning before me rushing to the bathroom to brush your teeth because you don't want me to smell your morning breath? That type of love when you want to be perfect in every aspect

You bring me my favorite lunch. You bring me my favorite candy and ice cream. On some Fridays, I discover hot Starbucks in my car with a rose on the dashboard and its petals in my coffee adding immense flavor to my favorite brew

It took almost a thousand years to find you. I didn't want to meet you due to the fear that you would be this perfect

We can pose for a photograph

We find ourselves on sandy Italian beaches and we vacation in Iceland, and bathe in the hot springs. Even the warmth of the natural volcano beneath us can't

The Facebook Status I Wish I Could Post

match your heat. I just want to sit here and wait for the Aurora Borealis to light up the sky

Your smile is captivating — utterly beautiful

Your voice incredibly, increasingly, invigoratingly rhythmic as it pulses with the twisting pattern of our conversation. Our thoughts collide and intellect intertwine, causing my cerebral cortex to pulse and release epinephrine molecules that are like a cacophony of narcotic opioids

Just by the substance and quality of our conversations and the union of vibrations I have been mentally fucked and satisfied.

My hypothalamus hasn't even been stimulated but my endocrine system goes to deliver a response to my reproductive system to induce the sexual arousal cascade to get a *"nutt"* …I think I need a cigarette already

Are you waiting for me at dawn when I come home from the office, because I can't wait to see you. Have you arisen before me to make my nappy-headed-ass breakfast in bed although you might view me as perfection

The Facebook Status I Wish I Could Post
Realizations

For some reason, I thought "*it*" was all wrong:

Being in love with another person rather it be a woman or a man. Being in love with a man — in love with a woman — not being fully happy. Or should I be in love with myself and adopt a child. I cringed at the fact of trying to see my future

Searching for answers I got in my knees and said, "Hail Mary Full of Grace", but they called me a sinner for I was *"Necromancing"*. But why when I had Jesus before anything

Lord forgive me, I know u wanna slap me

The Facebook Status I Wish I Could Post

My "song" song

I am the fortress you are the guard

When I am weak you are strong

I am the seasons you are the change in the weather

I am the symphony and you are the music to my heart

The Facebook Status I Wish I Could Post
Bite down

She looks at him. She hates the ways he looks at her. She loves everything about the way he looks at her. He is ugly. He is beautiful and utterly indescribable. Lips perfect, chin protracted by the gods. A muscular physique, deep innocent eyes that show his soul. Arms that embrace her body and giant hands that grab her ass on dark caerulean midnights that linger like the scent of vanilla extracts

Adagio's siren serenade was made

She pleasures him on her knees administering the deed. She runs his Nile River dry. Legs open at an angle his face goes in to pleasure her secret weapon. The perfect picture of him massaging her clitoris with his tongue

Her fire is burning, she inhaled deeply when his mouth was secured around her nipple

Making his way to her pelvis he bites just below her rib cage, and she falls into a deeper euphoria. The smell of marijuana and vanilla makes the room spin slowly and intensifies each stroke as he fucks her deep and hard, but with fiery passion. Her senses are in ash and his senses decimated

His thoughts race and ceases to exist. For in the process of an orgasm the desire has been completed by his lost forgotten wife. And hers by her long-forgotten husband

The Facebook Status I Wish I Could Post
Chase me

I wonder. . . how long?

How long will you continue to chase after me?

Every fiber in my body is telling me to let you in

But my heart is truly locked behind a fortress that is
almost impenetrable to few

I am truly learning to trust again but I keep taking the
lesson way to conceptually

You say you want my heart that's turned to stone but
what are willing to prove to pursue me?

You say way deep deep down that you care for me, but
you are not willing to be consistent

Can you take the time, instead of jumping to
conclusions?

Can you have patience with the broken hearted?

How long are you willing to wait?

Will there be a new engraved Rolex watch waiting for
me when I get home, matching relationship chains that
have the same quote that the tides and moon live by:
Push and Pull, King and Queen, or rose petals that lead
me to a steaming hot bath enriched with fresh oils?

Will you take me to the Waffle house on a Saturday
morning for a light breakfast or take me on a European
tour through Prague, Paris, Milan?

The Facebook Status I Wish I Could Post

God, I hope you choose Waffle house their sausage,
egg, and cheese wraps are to die for. Prague, Paris and
Milan can wait for the anniversary

Are you waiting for me in our New York City town
house with our dogs cooking dinner or at the Walmart
picking out my favorite ingredients, herbs, and spices?

Or maybe you're even getting my favorite wine — *our*
wine. The wine we had when we first met. It's hard to
find. Expensive and fermented since the 1977

Our friends are over at our town house, its Christmas
and we're sitting on the terrace enjoying a get-together
on a beautiful white Christmas day next to the fire pit.
Our guests are happy with the way they've been
entertained for the evening. The dogs are running
around the house as we're listening to Nat King Cole's
holiday music

These are the memories we'll create

You see I used to watch this perfect couple down in
central park. They were the embodiment of everything
I could ever want. It was like they were made for each
other. When she moved, he moved. When he spoke,
she finished his sentences

He absolutely couldn't let her hand go because if he
did she would be lost forever in time

They beckoned for one another like the earth needed
the sun — like the moon needed the earth to control the
tides

They waltzed in the park like no one was watching. I
envied them but it wasn't in a bad way

The Facebook Status I Wish I Could Post

They laughed and I could see the gleam in her eye like he had just given her Olympus and my god it was magnificent

All I could do was watch and cry to myself thinking I will never ever have what they have

Are you really the next person who is supposed to have me? How long are you willing to chase after me through the storm, the fire, the oceans the misty mountains? Would you cry for me, kill for me, die for me? Would you align your thoughts with mine, fight this war waging between our two worlds?

Chase me, please chase me cause when you finally catch me, *I* will truly be expressed…and in love.

The Facebook Status I Wish I Could Post
Ant Nests and Stairs

I dip my foot into a fire ant's nest

The colony swarms up my ankle biting and stinging

I tilt my head back and embrace the soothing pain

The fire and the burning sensation penetrate my veins; they burn but the pain is like soothing soft Egyptian silk.

Silk that's coursing through my veins up to my heart and through my aorta, and up into my mental cortex

I come to a place of reckoning and questions: Why do they not understand? Why do they not comprehend? Who am I... an imposter, a martyr, a pleaser, a thinker, a bitch, a pit? When I become myself, I will truly know

So far, all I see are blank walls that take me to the time I'm standing on wet beaches with an overcast sky. Tears streaming down my face and eyes red from crying. My beautiful body wrapped in *Our* Arabian ivory taffeta with the loose ends flowing in the wind

A crown adorns my head and I have my monarchy bearing down on my shoulders. The pressure is invisible, but in my mind, I am gasping for air trying to keep my head above the water. Although I know how to swim, I am terrified, and I can't calm my senses

My pupils constrict to their maximum potential. My neurotransmitters cause my axons to coil while I painfully reduce my stance to the fetal position. I can see the sun and the moon. My tides are thrashing

The Facebook Status I Wish I Could Post
against the seashore and my inner preservation is
softly eroding

After time the tides recede, I am here alone thinking to
myself: Abuser, timer, lover, singer, actor, releaser,
generator, illuminator, excavator, tempter, liner,
scepter, linger here oh sweet joy with sorrow

Those screams you want to let out are just on instant
replay in your head, but all you do is smile. You drink
a pint of water to flush out your body, but you're still
drunk from the alcohol trying to silence your pain: The
guilt, the shame, the hurt, the secrets. . . the fucking
torture, but I've heard Hell is worse so I'm not buggin

Waves bending. They are soothing. Push and pull were
their pattern. And might I say it is a lovely pattern they
love by. It is constant and never ending

I sigh and continue to use my Pestle, my mortar, my
pot, my kettle. I paint the ceiling, the floor, mop the
floor and petal my bike down long *"redundant"* roads.
Dancing rain and dancing seasons where are you my
love give me a reason…to stay here. Remember those
forgotten Thanksgivings and missed holidays; presents
unevenly exchanged on Xmas day

I think of you on empty bottle days when I'm drunk

Water, blood, sod, elixir, I don't drink the fluid of life
it's a deadly mixture. It brings death to wolves and
unhappiness to the innocent who find it

Fresh flower petals and add the meristem, and don't
forget those reminiscent memories of the pain that are
indelibly assorted on my mind

The Facebook Status I Wish I Could Post

Climbing stair in an abandoned house *i* wonder what awaits me on the highest floor. My eyes meet the sunset skies. A crown adorns my head. My monarchy is on my shoulders. How long will I continue to rule this country…my kingdom? My breath grows deeper each time I climb a stair. Times grows slower. And just as I come to the highest floor I return to the ant's nest in absolute happiness, wonder, and tears.

The Facebook Status I Wish I Could Post

Us

Us...well yes, we were in between worlds without end.

Walking in mazes, slaving for days, confused, and dazed.

Endless love making we prayed go away

Waiting for the new life, *our* new life to begin.

And when we met there between the trees on the verge of the sands, I knew from that point on our love was something no one else would understand.

The Facebook Status I Wish I Could Post

The End

www.ingramcontent.com/pod-product-compliance
Lightning Source LLC
Chambersburg PA
CBHW040853120626
46547CB00006B/588